I0459154

MONDAY WITH MOLLY

52 PEP TALKS TO KICKSTART YOUR WEEK

UNFILTERED FUEL FOR YOUR MOTIVATION, MOJO, AND MINDSET

MOLLY KENNEDY

Monday With Molly

Copyright © 2025 by Molly Kennedy

Paperback ISBN: 978-1-963732-16-0

Published by

The Publishing Pad
www.thepublishingpad.com

Picture: Jim Cielencki
Cover design: Jessi Elgersma, AHAP Media & Marketing Co.

Introduction

Monday hits hard. This book hits back.

Welcome to Monday with Molly. My hope for this book is to give some content, context, experience and perspective on all the different topics that you might be facing in your daily life. I've kept them short and sweet (like me) to make them enjoyable so you can start each week with a healthy mindset.

Monday With Molly is your weekly dose of real talk. 52 pep talks to help you reset your mindset and start the week strong. It's your go-to guide for weekly pick-me-ups and perspective shifts.

No sugar coating. Real, relatable advice to get you out of your own way, and keep showing up.

The foundation of every chapter in this book is based on the mindset skill I call Flip Your 20™. If you've read my first book, *Creating the Champion Within: How to get UP when life knocks you down*, heard any of my keynotes or follow me on Instagram or YouTube, you probably already know what Flip Your 20 is all about. If you're new here, consider this your Flip Your 20 101.

Life is all about perspective. It always has been, it always will be. There's a really fancy synonym for perspective. That word is paradigm. When you see this word for the first time, you may think it's pronounced like 'para dig em,' but it's pronounced like 'pair a dime'.

A pair of dimes equals 20 cents. Therefore, I nicknamed the word 'paradigm' 20 Cent. Your paradigm is your perspective. It's how you choose to see yourself, how you choose to see others, how you choose to see the world around you, how you choose to see what is possible for your future, how you choose to show up in your life every day. Your 20 Cent is the perspective, filter or lens you choose to look at the world through. It's a choice. Your choice. And your choice equals hope.

I love this word so much that I wear a pair of dimes as earrings, have a #flipyour20 tattoo, and my license plate says FLIPUR20. It's a lifestyle, grassroots movement and crusade I've been on for over 20 years.

There are two things that make your 20 Cent so powerful.

The first is that your 20 Cent only exists in one spot and that's in your brain. Nobody gets access up there unless you give it to them. Have you ever said something like, *she made me so mad, or he ruined my day?* We all have. Truth is no, he didn't, and no, she didn't. They said or did something, and you chose to get mad, and that's okay. I do, too. Please feel all the feelings. We're human. Please be human. Don't be perfect. Perfection is not a human quality. I'm just saying that starting today, choose to own whatever feelings you're having. The good, the bad, and the ugly. It's okay to be frustrated. That's normal. It's healthy. But don't blame someone else for making you feel bad. Maybe your past experience with the person is why you felt bad, or maybe you didn't get good sleep last night, or you're hungry, or just in a cranky mood. Whatever they said normally might be funny, but today you got ticked off. That's not them. It's you. It's how you choose to perceive it. It's your perspective of the situation.

And the beautiful thing about knowing your 20 Cent only exists in your brain is that you're 100% in control. You can only control what you can control. Nobody gets access up there unless you give it to them. They don't get to live in the penthouse where they're not paying rent. You know what I'm saying? When we start taking control of our responses and how we handle things, it puts us in the driver's seat. It doesn't matter your age; you could be 12, or you could be 82. You want to be in the driver's seat regardless of your age. So that's the first reason your 20 Cent is so powerful.

The second reason is that what you believe is what you get. Think about this right now in your own head. What do you believe is true about you? Your life? Your future? Your potential?

This may be the uncomfortable silence part. What do you believe is true about you? Take some time to search your heart and answer this question. I used to be a teacher, so I have good wait time. If what popped into your head for that question were awesome things like *I'm creative, fun, disciplined, hardworking, compassionate and empathetic...* that is amazing. Keep believing, doing and living more of that. However, I've asked this question enough to know that negative thoughts likely popped up for you first.

When I asked, "*What do you believe is true about you*"? were the thoughts that came into your head similar to, *I'm not good enough, I'm not smart enough, I'm not tall enough, short enough, pretty enough, creative enough, rich enough, etc.?* Some version of *I am not _____ enough*? Nod your head right now if this is true. If that's the case, you must first know you are not alone. You are not alone. Those negative thoughts are universal. It doesn't matter your age or how successful you are, we all have those limiting beliefs. But if that's your belief, be careful because what you believe is what you get. It's a self-fulfilling prophecy.

What if you were able to change that belief...on a dime? See what I did there? The great news is that you can. Flip Your 20 is THE skill that changes everything for the better.

Flip Your 20 is my play on words for paradigm shift. Paradigm is your 20 Cent. Flip Your 20 is shifting your paradigm. Get it? It's all about choosing to go from a negative perspective (tails) to an optimistic perspective (heads).

It's important to control the controllables because that is all we can do. Only you have access to your brain to be able to Flip Your 20. Flip Your 20 is simply answering the question: *Are you willing to see things from a different perspective? Are you willing to choose to see something positive instead of thinking you're not good enough?* Can you Flip Your 20? Instead of making negative confessions, say, *I am good enough. I've had some struggles. I know that people told me I'm not good enough, and maybe I started to believe that, but it's not true. I get to choose what I believe is true about myself moving forward.*

If you tell yourself something long enough, you believe it to be true. If someone else tells you something long enough, you believe it is true. I'm inviting you to question whether those limiting beliefs are true or not.

When is now a good time to Flip Your 20?

Flip Your 20 works in any situation, any day. It works at work, school, home, and in relationships—literally everything. You are the one in control of your 20 Cent, and you can Flip Your 20 and choose to see things differently at any time!

I love using athletes as an example. Imagine if Caitlin Clark is at the free-throw line at the end of a game and time has expired. Her team is down by one point. She gets two free throws and based on her performance, they win, lose or tie. If she gets to the free throw line and her 20 Cent (her perspective, her belief) is, *"Oh my gosh, I hope I don't miss. I hope I don't miss. Please don't miss, please don't miss, please don't miss…,"* there's a good chance she will miss because what she believes is what she gets.

Or, and hear me out. She could Flip Your 20 in that same situation. Everything leading up to that moment is identical, but if, in that moment, she chooses a different perspective, a different belief, and now her Flip Your 20 is, *"You're going to be sorry you fouled me. Cash money!"* There's a good chance she will make it.

This is why when you see elite-level athletes 'choke' at the end of a game, it's not because they are not skilled. It's because their belief and what they chose to focus on, in the moment, was what could go wrong. So it usually does.

However, when they Flip Your 20, and are in command of their mindset, you see them have ice in their veins at the end of a game. They have the supreme belief that it's going to go in. They're like, *give me the ball, coach.* The talent level may be the same, but the difference is in the moment. What's going on up in their brain? That's why they train their brain just as much, if not more, than their physical skill set. That's how powerful your 20 Cent is.

To master Flip Your 20, you must put in the reps. Practice in the most basic situations. If you have to wait 30 seconds in the drive-thru to get your coffee, don't honk your horn and get frustrated. Flip Your 20 and say to yourself, *"If this is the worst part of my day, I'm doing ok."* You choose the meaning you give to things. Everything is not that important and not a catastrophe. Try it today or the next time you have a tough meeting or presentation at work or a test at school.

Flip Your 20 is especially important if you get nervous or don't like to give presentations. If your belief is *"I always mess up. I'm probably going to mess up. It's going to be terrible,"* then yeah, it's going to be mediocre at best because that's what you believe and what you believe is what you get. Instead, you can Flip Your 20 and choose to believe, *"You know what? I have prepared as much as I possibly could. I know as much information as I can. I will go in with confidence and I will do the best that I can."* It's going to go better with this belief and a clear head. I don't know if it's going to be all-star or not, but I know it's not going to be horrible because you're prepared and you're confident. You'd be going with a sense of calm because you believe that you can.

I'll share a story for real-life context: I was keynoting at a state teen leadership conference in Michigan. A couple days later, I got a DM from a girl. She wrote, "I have to tell you, I wasn't sure if this Flip Your 20 thing really works or not." This is totally fair because it's a skill you have to put in the reps. Just like in the gym. She continued, "I didn't know if this would really work, but I thought I'd give it a shot." So she went to her competitive events, which they do at these kinds of conferences, and she writes, "I normally freak myself out. I get super nervous, I think of how much everyone is better than me. I usually kind of choke. But this time, I applied Flip Your 20." So she took action, she applied it, and then she DMs me and wrote, "Yeah, I mean, look, I was still a little nervous, but I wasn't panicky and I just thought, I can only control me. I am prepared. I have done the work, I know this stuff, and I can only control me."

She became the first female in her state's history to win gold in that competitive event because she heard a message, and took action on it. She believed in herself, which is the most important thing. Because she took action, she secured her spot at nationals. She created her own champion within and made history! This was the morning after she listened to my 30-minute keynote. That's how quickly Flip Your 20 works, if you work it.

You are not alone in your challenges and struggles. I've got your back and am cheering you on the whole way. Crack open these pages, find the pep talk you've been needing, and keep moving forward—one Monday at a time.

Keep this book somewhere you can easily access it—perhaps on your desk at work, in your car, in the restroom, or in your purse or messenger bag. Keep it close by.

Added bonus, if you need a little something to tie the end of the work week with a bow, you can reflect and answer the Flip Your 20 Friday question at the end of each chapter. Taking action is key.

Let's begin!

Week 1

Listen to wise, experienced people.

Regardless of your age, it's really important to seek out the perspective of other people who have different experience, more experience, and more wisdom than you to help you see things from a fresh perspective. I had this opportunity recently with a friend and someone who I have considered a mentor for a number of years now. She really helped me Flip Your 20 on how I see expanding my business and some of the roadblocks I was facing. She just completely flipped my perspective to see so many opportunities that are out there. She could do this for me because she has done the same in her life. She's shifted and changed and has always landed in the right spot for her. So no matter your age, seek out and reach out and listen to those who can open your eyes to see things from a wonderful, fresh perspective.

Flip Your 20.

What was your Flip Your 20 win this week?

_____

_____

_____

_____

_____

_____

_____

_____

_____

_____

_____

_____

_____

Week 2

Who is on your friend bookshelf?

One of the many amazing lessons I've learned from my therapist is that you have a bookshelf of friends and you get to choose at any time, at any age, who is on each shelf. On the top shelf are your top one or two, *maybe* three, friends whom you can go to at any time for any reason, especially when you're not at your best. And they can handle the situation, help you, and advise you. The bottom shelf is for friends who are there just for fun. Nothing serious, no deep conversations. You can have as many shelves as you want. We all evolve at different rates at different times in our lives. Sometimes we're stuck. Sometimes we know where we're going. So, based on where you are in your life, you get to choose and rearrange your bookshelf of friends at any time. And that's a good thing, but it can be hard as well. Just make sure you're taking care of you and you have the best people on the top shelf.

Flip Your 20.

What was your Flip Your 20 win this week?

_____

_____

_____

_____

_____

_____

_____

_____

_____

_____

_____

_____

_____

_____

Week 3

I wrote my own obituary…
it's not as morbid as you think.

I wrote my own obituary when I was 48. I love walking in
a beautiful cemetery in my city. I promise you it's not as
morbid as you might think. My obituary is really funny,
because I wrote it, just being honest. But I went through
a pretty traumatic experience at that time, and it made me
think that I have to update all of my affairs, make sure everything's in order, and not leave anything to chance. But
the real reason I'm sharing that is because once I wrote it,
how I wanted to be remembered, in my own words, it really
gave me an empowering position to then live that life, to
live it out, to make it come true. I often think that if this
were my last day or if I were on my deathbed, have I done
everything I wanted to do and have I become the person I
wanted to become? So I look at writing my own obituary as
a major Flip Your 20, not morbid, but empowering. Same is
true for you.

Flip Your 20.

What was your Flip Your 20 win this week?

_____

_____

_____

_____

_____

_____

_____

_____

_____

_____

_____

_____

_____

_____

Week 4

It feels good to not be miserable.

It feels great to not be miserable anymore. I was walking through my neighborhood, loving the beautiful trees that were in bloom. A woman walks by with her dog, and I say, "Oh, these trees are so beautiful." In an agitated tone, she responds, "Well, they don't last very long." And I thought, I'd hate to be in her head all day. Then I thought, huh, I used to be miserable for about 40 years. I can laugh now because I've done the work. I'm always talking about doing the work all the time. That's not just for working out. It's also doing the mental work, the emotional work, to heal, to move forward. I would not want to live in that woman's head. I would not want to live in my old head. I believe you wouldn't want to either, right? So be willing to get uncomfortable, do the work. You can choose to live in a beautiful state or a suffering state.

Flip Your 20.

What was your Flip Your 20 win this week?

_____

_____

_____

_____

_____

_____

_____

_____

_____

_____

_____

_____

_____

Week 5

Be willing to laugh at yourself.

Every time I'm at the grocery store, I put my food on the conveyor belt as if I'm going to win top prize for the most organized food on a conveyor belt. I watch my food going down the conveyor belt, and I have a little chuckle at my own expense. Same thing if you look in my kitchen cupboards. I like order. I like structure. It works for me most of the time. I was like, oh my gosh, I wonder, are people looking at this and thinking I'm a serial killer? Like, oh my gosh, she's crazy. Which is fine. I'm not really particularly concerned with what people think. But anyway, just one of those times to laugh at yourself. Check yourself sometimes too. Why do you do what you do? There's always a reason. By the way, there's no accidents when it comes to how we show up for ourselves. But anyway, that's a little insight into my grocery shopping.

Flip Your 20.

What was your Flip Your 20 win this week?

_____

_____

_____

_____

_____

_____

_____

_____

_____

_____

_____

_____

_____

Week 6

Tap into your JOMO!

Forget about FOMO. Tap into your JOMO: The Joy of Missing Out. I know that's not what everyone is saying, and I know that our comparison machines (aka smartphones) make us think that we have to do what everyone else is doing and have all the things and the money and the trips to keep up with the Joneses. Look, the Joneses are broke. Tap into the joy of missing out, meaning take a look at what you need to do to reach your goals, to feel inspired, to find peace, to find joy, to find excitement. You're not going to find it externally. Look inside your heart. Go inside your mind and say, maybe I need to miss out on some things that others are doing, so I can take time to focus on what I need to do to live my best life on my terms. Give it a try.

Flip Your 20.

What was your Flip Your 20 win this week?

_____

_____

_____

_____

_____

_____

_____

_____

_____

_____

_____

_____

_____

Week 7

Choose challenge over comfort.

Take the stairs instead of the elevator. Drink water instead of pop. Have the tough conversation instead of keeping it all in and stressing yourself out. Go to bed early and leave your phone outside the room. It's not easy, but you have to choose. We've been so programmed into finding the easy way, finding the comfortable way and look, me too. No judgment. But what if you choose to just get a little uncomfortable? Choose challenge over comfort because those small investments in your physical, mental, and overall health have a huge return on investment. Take on that challenge consistently and see the return on investment in your health. It's worth it.

Flip Your 20.

What was your Flip Your 20 win this week?

_____

_____

_____

_____

_____

_____

_____

_____

_____

_____

_____

_____

Week 8

**Create an environment that makes it
easier to reach your goals.**

I turned my dining room into my workout room, with a treadmill, weights, yoga mat, step-up box, etc. I want to get more steps in. I love walking, but I noticed I wasn't walking or going out for a walk as much in the evenings. I might just sit on the couch and be done for the day. So I turned my treadmill into a walking desk, and I put a shelf on it so I can get my work done. Several times, I've gone from taking a business call to watching WNBA Games and Women's College World Series. I can do anything from this walking desk. If I didn't buy this one little, simple shelf to make this a desk, I wouldn't be achieving all my health goals while doing my work. What is one simple change you can do to make your environment conducive for you to reach your goals? This might be easier than you think.

Flip Your 20.

What was your Flip Your 20 win this week?

_____

_____

_____

_____

_____

_____

_____

_____

_____

_____

_____

_____

_____

Week 9

If this is the worst part of your day…you're doing ok.

One time, my business brought me out to Portland, Oregon. I was super stoked to check off a new bucket list item: going to The Sports Bra. It's the first bar that only shows female sports on their TVs. Unfortunately, on the day I was to visit, I saw on social media that they had some water issues and were closed for the day. I thought to myself, if that's the worst part of my day, this thing I was totally looking forward to, if that's the worst part of my day, I'm doing all right because Flip Your 20 is a real-life skill. But here's a little serendipity. As I was taking a selfie outside The Sports Bra, the owner, Jenny, pulled up. She cashed in all her life savings to start this place that's now getting investments from Serena Williams' husband to franchise. Although I didn't get to go into the bar, I got to meet the owner. It's pretty epic to meet a badass woman like that. So when things don't go your way, you can Flip Your 20. Adapt. If this is the worst part of your day, you're doing all right.

Flip Your 20.

What was your Flip Your 20 win this week?

_____

_____

_____

_____

_____

_____

_____

_____

_____

_____

_____

_____

_____

Week 10

Think like Tarzan.

I recently had a friend give me some great advice as I'm trying to grow my business. He said, "Sometimes, just like Tarzan, when he wants to grab for that vine in front of him, he has to let go of the one behind him." OOF! That shook me. It got me thinking about another old saying, "What got you here won't get you there." I needed to let go of some old ways I've been doing things and get rid of some ego in order to have the courage to reach forward, grab that new vine, and keep moving forward. The same is true for you. What vine in your life do you need to let go of to move yourself forward, whether it's in your health, relationships, finances, goals, etc.? Be willing to let go of the old and grab the new vine because forward is a pace.

Flip Your 20.

What was your Flip Your 20 win this week?

_____

_____

_____

_____

_____

_____

_____

_____

_____

_____

_____

_____

Week 11

Your words are your most valuable currency.

Say what you mean and mean what you say. When you do this consistently, you build trust. You're showing the people in your life that you are dependable and they don't have to worry if you're going to follow through. It's just a given. Now, are there times you have to go back on your words? Sure. If some circumstance happens that you can't control or you're sick, of course. But in general, when you say what you mean and mean what you say and you follow through, trust goes through the roof. Nobody has to wonder if you're going to show up or do the thing you said you'd do. You have built that in, and that's a powerful way to connect with people. Choose to be a person of your word.

Flip Your 20.

What was your Flip Your 20 win this week?

_____

_____

_____

_____

_____

_____

_____

_____

_____

_____

_____

_____

_____

Week 12

Who will you set your alarm for?

My hiking friends and I do long hikes a few times a year. One of these hikes was a scheduled 20-plus miles. The alarm was set for 4:00 AM. I would absolutely set my alarm as early as needed for my hiking gal pals! Being out in nature, hearing the streams, our quiet times, and our really great talks replenish me. It refuels my soul. Those are the people I'll set my alarm for. Who will you set your alarm for? Or maybe you need to set your alarm for yourself, but what will you set it for? Is it to be out in nature? Is it to do your art or your music, or to cook, or to garden, or to learn whatever it is for you? Be willing to get up early to soak in the day in a way that refuels your soul. That's what I did that day. That's why 4:00 AM was a great start time. Give it a shot.

Flip Your 20.

What was your Flip Your 20 win this week?

_____

_____

_____

_____

_____

_____

_____

_____

_____

_____

_____

_____

Week 13

Vulnerability is strength.

Society has taught us that vulnerability is bad or a weakness, and I used to believe that lie myself. I'm sharing this because it reminds me of a Brene Brown quote where she says, "Share your story with those who have earned the right to hear it." And it makes me so grateful for the people I have in my life. Think about who you have in your life, whether it's family, friends, therapists—those top-shelf people who have earned the right to hear your story. Those people who you can be vulnerable with, who will be there to catch you, to love you, to advise you, to hold space for you. Think about how awesome that feels. We do that for others, but we have to be able to let others do that for us, too. It has to be a two-way street. I'm super grateful for the people in my life. And I hope you have your top-shelf people, too.

Flip Your 20.

What was your Flip Your 20 win this week?

_____

_____

_____

_____

_____

_____

_____

_____

_____

_____

_____

_____

_____

Week 14

Lessons learned from Simone Biles.

I was watching her documentary recently where she was talking about all the scrutiny she got when she pulled out of the vault during the Olympics because of the twisties. She said, "Especially with social media, it's okay to not be okay." We've heard it from Caitlin Clark recently, too. I'm sure you've heard that before. And I would third that. Look, being positive or having a positive attitude doesn't mean you're positive all the time. That's weird. Be willing to feel your feelings, all of them, the good, the bad, the ugly. Be positive or optimistic that you will get through it because you have people to turn to, to talk to, and you have healthy coping skills. My concern is that when we stop feeling, we definitely don't want that. So it's okay to feel icky. It's also okay to feel positive, but it's not about being positive all the time. It's okay to not be okay.

Flip Your 20.

What was your Flip Your 20 win this week?

_____

_____

_____

_____

_____

_____

_____

_____

_____

_____

_____

_____

Week 15

It's easy if you look for it.

Freudenfreude is finding joy in other people's joy. It is the opposite of what a lot of us do, schadenfreude, which is finding joy in other people's misery and pain. The Olympics is a great opportunity, although you can do it at any point. I watched one of my former students, Anita Alvarez, in her third Olympics for artistic swimming, formerly synchronized swimming. It was so cool. They did an upside-down moonwalk in the pool. It was amazing! Social media went wild with positive comments. And you saw the 2024 Olympics, when Simone Biles and Jordan Chiles bowed down to the Brazilian athlete, Rebeca Andrade. These are a couple of examples to find joy in other people's happiness and goodness, and celebrate it. Imagine if we did a little bit more of that, especially right now in the world. So I challenge you to have and practice some freudenfreude today.

Flip Your 20.

What was your Flip Your 20 win this week?

_____

_____

_____

_____

_____

_____

_____

_____

_____

_____

_____

_____

_____

Week 16

I used to think walking was dumb.

Yep. It wasn't a hard enough exercise or workout for me, so I thought it was a waste of time. I have since Flip Your 20. Obviously, we know all its health benefits, but for me, I really started to use it as a way to clear my head. Whether I'm having writer's block, brain fog, or frustrated about something, instead of just sitting and marinating in it, I get up and go for a walk. I may go outside or hop on my treadmill. I always come back with a clear head. So it just makes me want to ask you, what is that one, perhaps longstanding belief you have that it's time to reexamine?

Flip Your 20.

What was your Flip Your 20 win this week?

_____

_____

_____

_____

_____

_____

_____

_____

_____

_____

_____

_____

_____

Week 17

Remember to celebrate the small wins, too!

Remember to celebrate the small wins, especially when you're trying to achieve a big goal. Sometimes we wait until the finish line and celebrate it, or we wait for the big accomplishment along the way. That's cool. I get it. But as I've gotten older, I've learned that it's really important to celebrate the little successes along the way and to really celebrate the win, celebrate the heck out of it. Let's just take running, for example. If you would normally run 10 miles, but you *only* ran three, that's not an only. You ran three miles. Or instead of getting everything checked off your list, you *only* did two out of five items. Nope, you did two. When we celebrate the small ones that normally might not even register, we're training our brain to stack our successes and build momentum. And momentum matters.

Flip Your 20.

What was your Flip Your 20 win this week?

_____

_____

_____

_____

_____

_____

_____

_____

_____

_____

_____

_____

_____

Week 18

Boundaries are necessary.

Prentice Hemphill says, "Boundaries are the distance at which I can love you and me simultaneously." Brene Brown did research that found that the most wholehearted people and those with the highest self-respect have boundaries. So I'll give you a quick example. Here are two boundaries of mine. If you text me after 8:00 pm, you will probably not get a return message until the next day. It used to be 9:00 pm. It has been discussed and explicitly said because I don't have any friends who are mind readers. Another boundary is that I don't have FOMO. I have JOMO, the Joy of Missing Out. I hate group chats. So I have said to a group of people who do a lot of group chats that I would rather miss out on the fun opportunity to hang out and instead, see all the awesome pictures on Instagram, than be in a group chat. And I said that explicitly. They respect my boundary, and they don't put me in the group chat. It's awesome. Boundaries work. Give it a shot.

Flip Your 20.

What was your Flip Your 20 win this week?

_____

_____

_____

_____

_____

_____

_____

_____

_____

_____

_____

_____

Week 19

Make your brain a kind place to be.

You are the only one who lives up there, so make it a nice place to be. I'm sharing this because recently I came across some old journals and oh my gosh, OOF! I was so mean to myself, like brutal. Those journals were before therapy and dealing with all of my trauma and stuff. It makes me think about you. How many times do you say mean things about yourself in your own head that you would never say to anyone else? The saying goes, you would never talk to your friends the way you talk to yourself, or you probably wouldn't have any friends. Make today a new beginning, start fresh, renew. Why not use this time to little by little shift some of those negative thoughts into positive thoughts, or just be a little more gentle with yourself? Give yourself some grace and speak to yourself like you'd speak to a friend. Make your mind a kind place to be.

Flip Your 20.

What was your Flip Your 20 win this week?

_____

_____

_____

_____

_____

_____

_____

_____

_____

_____

_____

_____

_____

Week 20

Most people are good.

I get to travel all over the country as a professional speaker and author and I feel so grateful and fortunate that I get to meet so many awesome people. I mentioned on one of my Monday with Molly videos, with the news and the social media algorithm, it's easy to see the bad and the negative and all the hate. I choose to Flip Your 20, and be so grateful that I get to see the best in people, doing the work, helping each other, loving their job and making the future better. I get to see hope every single day, and I feel really grateful for that. So choose to look for the good because most people are good.

Flip Your 20.

What was your Flip Your 20 win this week?

_____

_____

_____

_____

_____

_____

_____

_____

_____

_____

_____

_____

_____

Week 21

Are you paying it forward?

I was working with a new teacher, and we were talking about how she wanted to change some things in her classroom, and some struggles she was having. I was able to share some advice from my years of teaching and working with teens. I reflected 20-plus years ago when a teacher I worked with shared some of her skills with me, which I used. Now I can pay it forward. This experience got me thinking that the whole goal of paying it forward is to help people struggle less than you did, right? I have no interest in seeing someone struggle, and I think, *well figure it out because I had to.* So is there something, no matter your age, that you're really good at? Do you have experience, a special skillset or niche in something? If you shared it with someone else who needs that information, it would help them struggle less and succeed quicker or feel more confident in what they're doing. That's a really good thing to do. Are you doing it?

Flip Your 20.

What was your Flip Your 20 win this week?

_____

_____

_____

_____

_____

_____

_____

_____

_____

_____

_____

_____

_____

Week 22

What advice would you give your younger self?

I was pondering this question, and two things came up for me. One, I would have asked for help sooner. I didn't really do it until I was 35. That was when I asked for help and went to therapy. This was an EPIC game changer for my life. The second piece of advice would be to worry less. I did not realize I was such a worrier, but it makes sense. Everything kept going wrong for me when I was younger. I was always in survival mode. Now, I have trained my brain to Flip Your 20, do the work, and the therapy. I can look back on those two things and say, man, those would've been a game changer. So what is it for you? It doesn't matter how old you are, what advice would you give your younger self? And are you currently taking that advice to move you forward?

Flip Your 20.

What was your Flip Your 20 win this week?

_____

_____

_____

_____

_____

_____

_____

_____

_____

_____

_____

_____

_____

Week 23

Mute Monday.

Today is Mute Monday. This is something I do every once in a while when I notice myself feeling icky, frustrated or comparing myself to others when I leave someone's social media. I'll mute or unfollow them. I think it's a great self-care tip. I encourage you to do the same. Social media can be used for a lot of great things. You can feel empowered or inspired, and I hope I do that on my social media. That's my goal. But I'm certainly not everybody's cup of tea, so if you don't like what I'm posting, please mute and unfollow me. I think it's a healthy thing to find your people, to find the message that really resonates with you. There's enough noise going on in the world, so get your algorithm to work for you on Mute Monday.

Flip Your 20.

What was your Flip Your 20 win this week?

_____

_____

_____

_____

_____

_____

_____

_____

_____

_____

_____

_____

_____

Week 24

Thumper's mom was right.

If you don't have anything nice to say, don't say anything at all. There's a lot of noise in the world right now. Like A LOT, A LOT. It's intense. So it's okay to practice some self-restraint by not arguing or getting into arguments online or in person. Have the self-discipline so you can rest your head at night with a clear conscience. At least that's my perspective right now. Also, the flip side of what Thumper's mom was saying, I think, is if you do have something nice to say, say it. That means thank you, you're welcome, saying hi to someone. Words like, thanks for helping me out or great job in the game last night. Whatever it is, those are perhaps even more important right now. Choose to do more of that.

Flip Your 20.

What was your Flip Your 20 win this week?

_____

_____

_____

_____

_____

_____

_____

_____

_____

_____

_____

_____

_____

Week 25

Do hard things on purpose.

When I'm on a road trip, I like to find cool outdoor things to do if I'm in a new place. While on a trip to a friend's hometown, she suggested that I do the dune climb, which means climbing a couple of hills in sand. I love climbing, but sand makes it harder. So was I out of breath? Yep. Was it hard? Yep. But did I love it? Yep. Because I've trained my brain to want to do difficult things, so I can get stronger physically and mentally. And it was raining. I had to wait out the rain. I hoped it didn't rain again. But that's another little element of challenge. Be willing to put yourself in situations that are safe, but still challenging, so you can show up as that new version of yourself. It's worth it.

Flip Your 20.

What was your Flip Your 20 win this week?

_____

_____

_____

_____

_____

_____

_____

_____

_____

_____

_____

_____

_____

Week 26

Delayed gratification before you buy.

Delayed gratification is strength. I'm sharing this one because I got an Instagram ad for an item that I thought would be fun and cool. But at the time I didn't need that thing. I am not an impulsive shopper. I don't really buy things right away. I'm just not wired that way. So I did my research, looked at different sites, different brands, different stores, etc. I waited to make that decision. After that pause, I didn't feel like buying it anymore. Shortly after that, I watched the Netflix show called "Buy Now." It's a documentary that illustrates how manipulative marketing is when it comes to consumerism. So, before you pay for that item, just maybe ask yourself if you really need it. Put it in your cart. Wait a little bit. If it's not something you need, remove it from your cart. Try delayed gratification this week.

Flip Your 20.

What was your Flip Your 20 win this week?

_____

_____

_____

_____

_____

_____

_____

_____

_____

_____

_____

_____

_____

Week 27

Safety is at the core.

I was speaking with one of my friends recently. We were trying to brainstorm ways to help one of her students become regulated in class because he came from a really tough home life. As we were brainstorming, I told her that one of the key things I'd recommend as a person who has been through plenty of trauma is that safety is at the core. Anything she tries to implement needs to meet the most fundamental criteria: the child has to feel safe. There has to be some level of trust, and there must be routine, which my friend creates because she's an awesome teacher. The same is true for you. If you've been through some stuff in your life or the people in your life have, the most important thing you can do for you or them is create a safe space. So when someone's in your presence, do your best to create that space where they feel some level of safety. Leave people better than you find them.

Flip Your 20.

What was your Flip Your 20 win this week?

_____

_____

_____

_____

_____

_____

_____

_____

_____

_____

_____

_____

Week 28

What elevates your JOY meter?

For me, it's snow, cold and winter gear. Oh my gosh, I love it so much. It's been so long since we had a solid winter where I live. I love going outside to enjoy it. It's so beautiful. I geek out. Everybody I've met on a snowy trail was happy and kind. We end up laughing and feeling at peace. It's so beautiful and tranquil in the snow. And I would also say, when I did 23 and Me, besides being Irish, they said I was approximately 30% Italian and a small percentage from Sicily. I think they missed my Scandinavian roots. How can I not be from Finland? I'm just saying. Snow, cold and winter gear are what elevate my joy meter. I come alive in the winter. Alright, I love this for me. Find out what elevates your joy meter and do more of that.

Flip Your 20.

What was your Flip Your 20 win this week?

_____

_____

_____

_____

_____

_____

_____

_____

_____

_____

_____

_____

Week 29

Always keep it real reel.

2024 was a really difficult year for me. Perimenopause kicked my butt physically, mentally and emotionally. I felt like a shell of myself. It was a really, really hard year. I was finally able to get back up to the Adirondack Mountains in the north country of New York State. Hiking a couple of smaller peaks made me so grateful for awesome friends, empathetic doctors, my wonderful therapist, effective meds and healthy coping mechanisms to help me keep going. It's like that song, "If you're going through hell, keep on going." That's kind of what 2024 was for me. So to be back up in the mountains and to get some hikes in felt exhilarating. My stamina was not where it usually is, but I celebrated the heck out of it because it was way more than I could have imagined. It was certainly better than the past summer when I could barely get off the couch. Don't be ashamed of your real reel. Celebrate it. You're not alone. Keep on going. Forward is a pace.

Flip Your 20.

What was your Flip Your 20 win this week?

_____

_____

_____

_____

_____

_____

_____

_____

_____

_____

_____

_____

_____

Week 30

Sometimes it's best to simply listen.

I'm sharing this because I recently passed through customs, and the border agent asked what I did for work. I told her I am a professional speaker and author, and I've spent many years working with teens. She asked, *Do you have five minutes?* I was thinking, well, you have my ID, and there's no one behind me in line. LOL. She starts telling me about her family. She's trying to teach her son about being resilient and avoiding coddling him and all the teenage things. And she was doing a great job, actually. I added a couple fillers like, wow, that's great, yes. But most of the time I just sat there quiet, making eye contact, holding a safe space for her. She felt compelled, for whatever reason, to open up and share all these things with me, a stranger. My job was simply to listen. The key is to read the room. Sometimes people just need you to hold space for them so they can share whatever they need to share. Focus on listening more this week.

Flip Your 20.

What was your Flip Your 20 win this week?

_____

_____

_____

_____

_____

_____

_____

_____

_____

_____

_____

_____

_____

_____

Week 31

Eat the damn cookie!

This is for anyone who is either currently or has ever dealt with any sort of issues around food or body image. I'm certainly raising my hand to that. Halloween through New Year's Day is the time of year when social media will try to shame you or guilt you into feeling bad. You'll see posts like *if you eat the apple pie, you have to run X number of minutes*. No, you don't. So you know what, social media…#shutyourface. If enjoying the sweets or extra servings around the holidays brings you joy, go for it. It's really not that big of a deal. Or if it's another time of the year, as long as most of the time your lifestyle is just moving your body and eating pretty well, you're good. Trust me, you're good. So don't let social media guilt you or make you feel bad about celebrating with food at the holidays. Eat the damn cookie.

Flip Your 20.

What was your Flip Your 20 win this week?

_____

_____

_____

_____

_____

_____

_____

_____

_____

_____

_____

_____

_____

Week 32

Shame rarely leads to change.

In case you're encroaching on a new habit or new goal this year, instead of shaming yourself, do these three things. First, give yourself some grace. You're starting from where you're starting. Whether it's the first time or the 10th time, it doesn't matter. Two, create an environment that allows you to be successful. If you're trying to work out more, pack your gym bag and put it by the door before you go to bed. You're not packing it in the morning. Let's be honest! And then the third and final thing is to celebrate every small win. Because every time you keep a promise to yourself and do the new behavior, that is a WIN. I don't care how tiny, celebrate the heck out of it.

Flip Your 20.

What was your Flip Your 20 win this week?

_____

_____

_____

_____

_____

_____

_____

_____

_____

_____

_____

_____

Week 33

The Human Factor.

There's a quote going around social media saying something to the effect of *artificial intelligence is here to stay, but there's no such thing as artificial humanity.* I love that because here's the thing, what if we just choose to show up for each other and let people know that we see them, they're valuable and they matter. That's what the human factor is. We are holding a space for people when we say things like: "Hey, you've been on my mind." "I'm checking in." "Congrats on the goal." "I'm so sorry you're going through this tough time." "I'm here to support you in whatever way you need." Hold a safe space to allow them to simply be and to be seen without judgment. That's the human factor. Let's do more of that because we all need it.

Flip Your 20.

What was your Flip Your 20 win this week?

_____

_____

_____

_____

_____

_____

_____

_____

_____

_____

_____

_____

_____

Week 34

March Madness.

I love March Madness. Just like a lot of people, I filled out a bracket. I love watching the games, the buzzer beaters, the upsets, and the Cinderella stories. We put a lot of time and energy looking up the scores and losing productivity during this time. And look, me too. It makes me think, what about filling out your own bracket for you? Maybe you have a bracket about sleep hygiene, and it's you going to bed at a certain bedtime vs. you scrolling until 2:00 AM. Which action won? Or you're eating a bunch of junk food vs. healthy food. Which action won? Or you decide to get up when the alarm goes off the first time, vs. you letting it go off five times. Which action won? I'm simply saying, let's put the same enthusiasm and vigor into our own lives because that really matters, too.

Flip Your 20.

What was your Flip Your 20 win this week?

_____

_____

_____

_____

_____

_____

_____

_____

_____

_____

_____

_____

Week 35

I'm convinced it's the little things that matter most.

I am convinced more and more that it's always the little things that matter and make a difference. Recently, I was dropping my car off at the airport, getting ready for an early morning flight. It was dark out. I saw the shuttle bus all the way at the other end of the parking lot. Out of nowhere, the driver flashes the lights, puts the left turn signal on, indicating that there are parking spaces near her. So I flashed my lights at her like, okay. She did it again and I went right to where she was. There was an easy parking spot, and I said, *that was so nice of you to do that.* She said, "I do it all the time. I didn't know that you noticed. You don't need to keep looking around. Let me help you." And I thought it really is the little things. She could have just sat there, but she chose to help. It doesn't take a lot to have a big impact. So focus on doing those little things consistently.

Flip Your 20.

What was your Flip Your 20 win this week?

_____

_____

_____

_____

_____

_____

_____

_____

_____

_____

_____

_____

_____

Week 36

Just be YOU!

Please don't be fake. I'm sharing this because I was recently speaking with some students, and they came up after and said, "Thank you for just being authentic and keeping it real. Like you totally get us. And a lot of adults say they're going to keep it real, and they totally don't." That's great feedback to hear. I love it and I'm sharing it because in order to have any sort of meaningful connection or relationship, I don't care what age you are, or where you come from, nobody wants to deal with fake people. We've learned to fake it from social media. But in real life, the human factor is just to show up and be you. That's what your gift is. I've said this before, I'm the gray-haired, no makeup, jacked-up lady. Cool. That's who I am. And it's real. And that's why my message resonates with teens. Just be you.

Flip Your 20.

What was your Flip Your 20 win this week?

_____

_____

_____

_____

_____

_____

_____

_____

_____

_____

_____

_____

_____

Week 37

It's NEVER too late.

In the same month, I received two compliments that I have never received in the past, certainly not before therapy, probably not even before a few years ago. So for anyone who knows me from a long time ago, brace yourself. You know you would never identify me this way. Neither would I. I had one person, a teacher friend of mine say, "You are one of the sweetest people I know." Soon after that, I sat next to a woman on an hour-long flight. As we were landing, she said, "You have such a calming presence. Normally I take my anxiety meds because I hate flying and I'm a total wreck. But on this trip, we just talked the whole time." Of course, I told her about Flip Your 20. I'm sharing this because I was like *I have a calming presence?* If you know the older version of me, that's not how anyone would have described me. Time helps and therapy heals. It's never too late. Do the work.

Flip Your 20.

What was your Flip Your 20 win this week?

_____

_____

_____

_____

_____

_____

_____

_____

_____

_____

_____

_____

_____

Week 38

How long until you learn your lesson?

It has taken me close to 51 years to learn two lessons in the same week. The first was when I started to feel sick. Instead of waiting and waiting and waiting and waiting, I went to the doctor right away, got a diagnosis of a viral infection and was able to treat it right away. This was a major win for me. The second lesson is that I actually listened to my body, and I rested a lot over that week. And I can say that a week later, I was feeling close to normal. I was able to sleep again, and I got some of my energy back. So, it took me almost 51 years to learn to listen to my body and not be so darn stubborn. I would encourage you to please have a shorter learning curve.

Flip Your 20.

What was your Flip Your 20 win this week?

_____

_____

_____

_____

_____

_____

_____

_____

_____

_____

_____

_____

Week 39

Less 'just' and 'only.'

I invite you to remove the words just and only from your vocabulary in certain contexts because they diminish you and your goals. Let's stop that. For example, I only ran a 5K. Nope, you ran a 5K. That's amazing. Or I'm just a mom. Just a mom? You're raising a human being. That's wild! That's amazing. Or I can only play an easy song on the piano. You can read music and play the piano? That is amazing. Wow! See what I'm doing here? We have these goals, or we achieve a thing, or we try to make progress, and then we immediately diminish them by using 'just' or 'only'. I highly encourage you to remove those or catch yourself when you say them, and say them less. I'm telling you it makes a big difference.

Flip Your 20.

What was your Flip Your 20 win this week?

_____

_____

_____

_____

_____

_____

_____

_____

_____

_____

_____

_____

Week 40

Discipline = Freedom.

Discipline equals freedom. Meaning if you discipline yourself, like I have for the past few decades, to create a habit to move my body every day, you'd have the freedom to accomplish any physical goal you set. I love doing stairs, and although they are never easy, they help me build more physical and mental strength. Don't wait until you're motivated. You'll be waiting forever. So think about this for you. The discipline to save money gives you financial peace. That's freedom. The discipline to say no to the fun thing and do the hard thing first gives you the freedom and enjoyment when you're doing the fun things after you've gotten the hard stuff done first. What is one area of your life where you can be more disciplined this week? Your future self will thank you for it. Discipline equals freedom. Do the work.

Flip Your 20.

What was your Flip Your 20 win this week?

_____

_____

_____

_____

_____

_____

_____

_____

_____

_____

_____

_____

_____

Week 41

Be willing to be a beginner.

Maybe you're amazing in one area and you're trying something new in another area, but you're so frustrated because you stink at it. That's okay. Or maybe you're upping your level in something, but you're a beginner at the next level. It can be frustrating, but that's okay, too. I'm sharing this because I'm embarking on expanding my business, and there are some new things I have to learn that make me feel like a beginner. And it's hard. There are certainly times of struggle, and oh my gosh, it's so frustrating at times. And because multiple things can be true at the same time, I choose to find it exciting and exhilarating. And I love having to be so disciplined and laser-focused and obsessed with something until it becomes easier. Then I'm not a beginner anymore. Keep that in mind as you're working on whatever your new thing is; you have to start somewhere.

Flip Your 20.

What was your Flip Your 20 win this week?

_____

_____

_____

_____

_____

_____

_____

_____

_____

_____

_____

_____

_____

Week 42

Reflect, celebrate and evolve.

Remember to reflect on how far you have come. Sometimes when we're in it, we forget to look around and reflect and think, *wow, I've come really far.* Or *I would've handled that situation really poorly in the past, but now I handled it better. Oh my gosh! That is some serious growth and evolution.* I share this because I'm at a point in my life where, personally and professionally, I am in a big growth and evolution moment. And it feels really good. It's exciting. It also causes nervousness. Sometimes it is overwhelming, but I can also look back and say, I overcame a lot before. I'm sure the same is true for you. I believe that challenges are gifts, and that keeps me moving forward. Choose to reflect on how far you've come and have a clear vision of where you want to go next. It's not easy, but it's always worth it.

Flip Your 20.

What was your Flip Your 20 win this week?

_____

_____

_____

_____

_____

_____

_____

_____

_____

_____

_____

_____

_____

Week 43

It's better to belong than it is to fit in.

Belonging is about knowing who you are and showing up as your true, authentic self. It's about how you speak, dress, act, etc. Regardless of the situation you're in, you're just fully you, and the right people will be drawn to you. You're not for everybody, and that's okay. The opposite of belonging is fitting in, which a lot of us did when we were younger. Perhaps we still do even as adults. Fitting in is essentially changing who you are, how you speak or dress or show up, depending on the situation you're in and the people you're with. We do this chameleon shift so they like us. When you choose to fit in, essentially you're betraying yourself, and that's not okay. Choose to belong...to you.

Flip Your 20.

What was your Flip Your 20 win this week?

_____

_____

_____

_____

_____

_____

_____

_____

_____

_____

_____

_____

Week 44

Remember to take your own best advice.

Give yourself some grace and space. That was one of the best pieces of advice I received from a friend after my grandpa passed away. I was trying to fight through the grief, and he said, "You have got to give yourself some grace and space," and it just hit me. I was like, yeah, I need to be kind and gentle with my emotions and energy as I work through it. That's been a piece of advice I've given to plenty of people over the years. I had a really rough day recently. As I was talking to a friend about it, one of the first things she said was, "I think you're being too hard on yourself, you need to give yourself some grace and space." I thanked her for saying that. Sometimes we need to hear our own advice because when we're in it and we're frustrated or distracted, it's hard to think clearly. So make sure you're taking your own best advice as well. Give yourself some grace and space.

Flip Your 20.

What was your Flip Your 20 win this week?

_____

_____

_____

_____

_____

_____

_____

_____

_____

_____

_____

_____

Week 45

My go-to mantra during physical challenges.

I tell myself, *thank you body, thank you mind,* in a very gentle tone when I'm facing any physical challenge. I started doing it during the pandemic, when I was so grateful for my health. I'm sharing this because two friends and I did a 50-mile backpacking challenge. We were carrying all of our gear, food, and shelter in our pack that weighed 20 to 30 pounds. We had 48 hours and camped for two nights. At one point we were like, this isn't fun. It wasn't fun, fun, but it was cool. And I felt good most of the time. And then there were some moments where I was like, okay, I'm done. Yet I chose to keep going, and I loved it. I love spending time in the woods. Some points were tough, frustrating, and I felt a painful blister or two forming on my feet. But instead of focusing on that, I chose to bring my attention back to my mantra. *Thank you body, thank you mind.* And it helped me to keep moving forward, especially when it was tough. So give it a shot when next you're facing your own physical challenge.

Flip Your 20.

What was your Flip Your 20 win this week?

_____

_____

_____

_____

_____

_____

_____

_____

_____

_____

_____

_____

_____

Week 46

Be open to receiving feedback.

It's not always easy. Sometimes we take it personally, or we get offended. Of course, it depends on the delivery as well. I have a friend who had an upcoming presentation and she was asking a bunch of people for feedback. It made me think that sometimes when we're giving feedback, it's way easier, of course, because we're being gentle and nice. But on the flip side, when we either ask for feedback or it's given to us from, again, people we trust, not some haters or trolls, we need to be open to it. Just pause for a second and ask yourself if there's any truth in what they've shared. Or say, "Oh, I didn't see it from that perspective." Be willing to see if there's a way you can adjust. It's not always easy, but it is important to be open to it.

Flip Your 20.

What was your Flip Your 20 win this week?

_____

_____

_____

_____

_____

_____

_____

_____

_____

_____

_____

_____

_____

Week 47

Fly your freak flag!

I was visiting a high school where I knew a bunch of the kids. Two boys sprint around the corner, and they're coming down the hall, full steam ahead. I said, "Whoa, guys, chill, chill, chill." They kind of slowed down, but they kept walking towards me, kind of goofing around. I knew one of the boys who was often in trouble (aka frequent flyer), but I didn't know the other boy. So the kid I know says, "Oh, she's jacked. You're the muscle chick, right? You're the muscle chick!" So I pat my biceps. I'm like, obviously, oh my God, thank you. So they keep walking towards me, then the boy I know says to the kid I don't know, "Oh, she's going to keep me safe, man. She's jacked."

As they come closer, I say to the kid I don't know, "Come here!" Well, he bolts down the stairs and I said, "Yeah, you better run." LOL! I'm sharing this because this speaks to my freak flag. Society says that is not how a 50-year-old woman acts. Well, that's how I act. If the frequent flyer kid says I'm the muscle chick, and wants to come to me for safety, I'm going to plant that flag and fly it. So fly your freak flag with pride.

Flip Your 20.

What was your Flip Your 20 win this week?

_____

_____

_____

_____

_____

_____

_____

_____

_____

_____

_____

_____

_____

Week 48

Is your mindset like a spring dandelion?

Dandelions pop up everywhere in the spring. They are contagious. When the white puffy part blows and spreads all over, it creates even more weeds. I think a lot of us have mindsets like the spring dandelions, where even when you cut them down, they come back up because we're choosing to focus on what is going wrong, bad, or unfair. Focusing on the negative means you'll keep spreading more negative, just like the weeds. Instead, you can choose to Flip Your 20 and act like one of those lawn care treatment places. Of course, we're going to say, let's keep it organic because we want to take care of Mother Earth. We know that the bad thoughts, the 'dandelions', are still under there, but we're going to control them by putting healthy thoughts on top. We can choose to keep feeding our minds positive, optimistic, resourceful thoughts to keep the negative ones at bay. They're still going to pop up from time to time, but you get to choose when.

Flip Your 20.

What was your Flip Your 20 win this week?

_____

_____

_____

_____

_____

_____

_____

_____

_____

_____

_____

_____

_____

Week 49

Feel ALL of your feelings.

I love climbing stairs for exercise. It helps me clear my mind. I was doing some deep reflection on my life, where I've been, where I am, and where I'm going. I just got super overwhelmed and started to cry for 10 or 15 minutes. It was a combination of sadness, grief, joy, and pride. It felt like it came out of nowhere. And that's okay. You're allowed to feel your feelings. You're human. It's healthy. The concern comes in when we numb our feelings and choose not to feel at all. That's not okay. So keep being honest and real with yourself. I'm putting this out here because you don't see a lot of this on social media. It's all highlight reel stuff. This is the real reel. So turn to the people who care about you, love you, and support you. Always know that you're never alone.

Flip Your 20.

What was your Flip Your 20 win this week?

_____

_____

_____

_____

_____

_____

_____

_____

_____

_____

_____

_____

_____

Week 50

Be bold and go for it!

Be willing to take the risk, be brave, and just do the thing. I entered a speaking competition in Florida, where I competed against people from all across the United States. A whole bunch of people auditioned virtually. One hundred and twenty people were selected. I earned my way into the top 30, but missed out on making it into the top 10. Although it was disappointing, I'm also proud. You can be two things at the same time. Always remember that. As I rested and recovered, I remembered the saying, "It's about the journey and not always the goal or the destination." It's cliche, but usually cliches are true. So I feel really proud of myself. 2024 was my year of yes. The year to make bold decisions. I hope that inspires you. Even when something's really hard, just go for it anyway. Be bold, be brave, and stand in your power.

Flip Your 20.

What was your Flip Your 20 win this week?

_____

_____

_____

_____

_____

_____

_____

_____

_____

_____

_____

_____

_____

Week 51

Recognize when it's just not your day.

I don't know about you, but sometimes I'm just not fit for human consumption. I'm sharing this because a friend called me recently. She was talking about some personal things and needed a productive vent. I'm usually a great listener. I'm very empathetic. Oof, that day I was in a foul mood, and I didn't realize it until I noticed how I was responding. It did not sound like me, and I was not being very helpful. I said, "I don't know what's wrong with me today, I'm just pissy. Please know that I'm not judging, and this is clearly the worst advice I've ever given you." I acknowledged and owned it. And fortunately, she was very kind and gracious, and I apologized again later. The point is, sometimes you just have to recognize when it's just not your day. And that's ok.

What was your Flip Your 20 win this week?

_____

_____

_____

_____

_____

_____

_____

_____

_____

_____

_____

_____

_____

Week 52

Time helps, and therapy heals.

I started therapy in March of 2009. As I write this, it's been a little over 16 years since that first appointment. Thank goodness I finally asked for help at 35 years old. My friend referred me, and I am very grateful to have found my therapist on the first try. She helped me completely change the trajectory of my life. Oftentimes you'll see me on social media encouraging you to do the work when it comes to workouts, like physically do the work. Similarly, I can assure you there are no shortcuts to mental and emotional fitness and healing. You must do the work. A lot of times it's hard and ugly, and you may want to quit, but you must keep going if you want to get to the other side. And I have to say, I'm always impressed by how resilient our bodies are. I don't know how my body physically handled all the stress, anger and resentment I carried for decades, but it did somehow. I want to share with you that time helps, but therapy heals. Do the work.

Flip Your 20.

What was your Flip Your 20 win this week?

_____

_____

_____

_____

_____

_____

_____

_____

_____

_____

_____

_____

_____

_____

Conclusion

You made it here. You made it happen. Monday after Monday, you took the lead and showed up for yourself. You stared down a year of Mondays, coming out stronger on the other side. This book was never about perfection; it was about progress and learning that forward is a pace. Keep trusting your gut. Lean into that start-of-the-week self-doubt because you are rolling with a fresh perspective these days. You've got the tools. You've got the fuel. You're on the Flip Your 20 train. Now go make your Mondays, and your mindset, count. I'm here to cheer you on!

I would love to hear about how you're using Flip Your 20 in your everyday life. Let's connect on Instagram @ flipyour20_ and on YouTube @Molly Kennedy. Cheers to an amazing week.

About the Author

Molly is an award-winning international keynote speaker and a specialist in mindset, perseverance, and human connection, but let's get real: she didn't start out that way.

For most of her life, Molly fought with feelings of worthlessness, carried a chip on her shoulder, and was a full-time lone wolf.

After clocking some serious hours in therapy, building a community of fantastic friends, and gathering a steady stream of personal pep talks, Molly flipped her mindset and her life's work.

She walks the walk when it comes to resiliency, grit and perseverance. Molly grew up in a dysfunctional family marked by addiction, divorce, abuse, neglect, and abandonment. She struggled with an eating disorder, was suicidal and became a runaway at 15.

If you're looking for a powerful message about overcoming obstacles, reaching goals and creating the best version of yourself, Molly is your speaker!

Molly only asks others to challenge themselves because she has done that her entire life. She's a bodybuilding champion, an Empire State Games gold medalist in Olympic-style weightlifting, a full Ironman Triathlon finisher (140.6 miles), and a multiple-time marathoner. She has jumped out of an airplane twice, walked across fire twice, climbed the equivalent of Mt. Everest in 32 hours and summited all 46 of New York State's highest mountains.

Molly has the street cred and lived experience to help elevate you to your summit. LET'S GO!

www.ingramcontent.com/pod-product-compliance
Lightning Source LLC
Chambersburg PA
CBHW061658120626
46550CB00003B/995